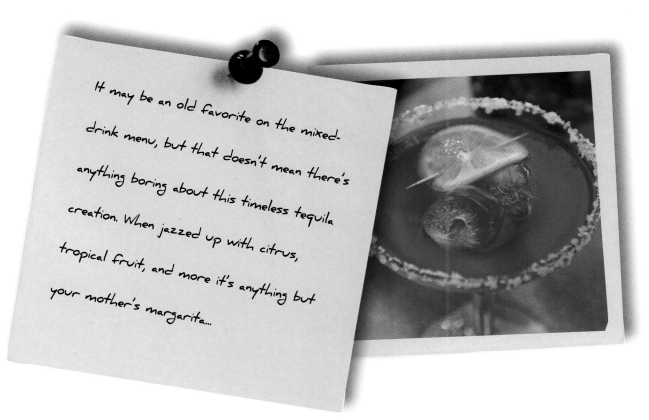

It may be an old favorite on the mixed-drink menu, but that doesn't mean there's anything boring about this timeless tequila creation. When jazzed up with citrus, tropical fruit, and more it's anything but your mother's margarita...

MARGARITA
now you're cookin'
PARTY

THIS BOOK JUST MAKES YOU WANNA COOK.

REBO
PUBLISHERS

© 2003 Rebo International b.v. Lisse, The Netherlands

This edition printed in 2010.

Original recipes, photographs, and design: © R&R Publications
Marketing Pty. Ltd., Victoria, Australia

Cover design: Minkowsky Graphics, Enkhuizen, The Netherlands
Typesetting: Artedit Typographic Studio, Prague, Czech Republic
Proofreading: Erin Ferretti Slattery, Elizabeth Haas

ISBN 978 90 366 2525 8

MARGARITA
PARTY

now you're cookin'

Foreword

Perfect year-round but especially in the summer, margaritas are popular, refreshing, ice-cold drinks with a citrus and tequila zing. This book has all you need to put together a Margarita Party celebrating all different kinds of margaritas and the best appetizers to accompany them.

From classic and frozen margaritas to tequila drinks, *Now You're Cookin' Margarita Party* offers a great variety of recipes to make your party fun and unique, with over thirty margarita recipes and over a dozen recipes for appetizers.

Try the Traditional Margarita, the Cadillac Margarita, or the Cowboy Margarita paired with zesty appetizers such as Beef Braised in Rioja, Chicken Meatballs in Sweet Chili Sauce, and Baby Octopus Marinated in Olive Oil and Oregano. You're sure to enjoy this array of enticing drinks and snacks.

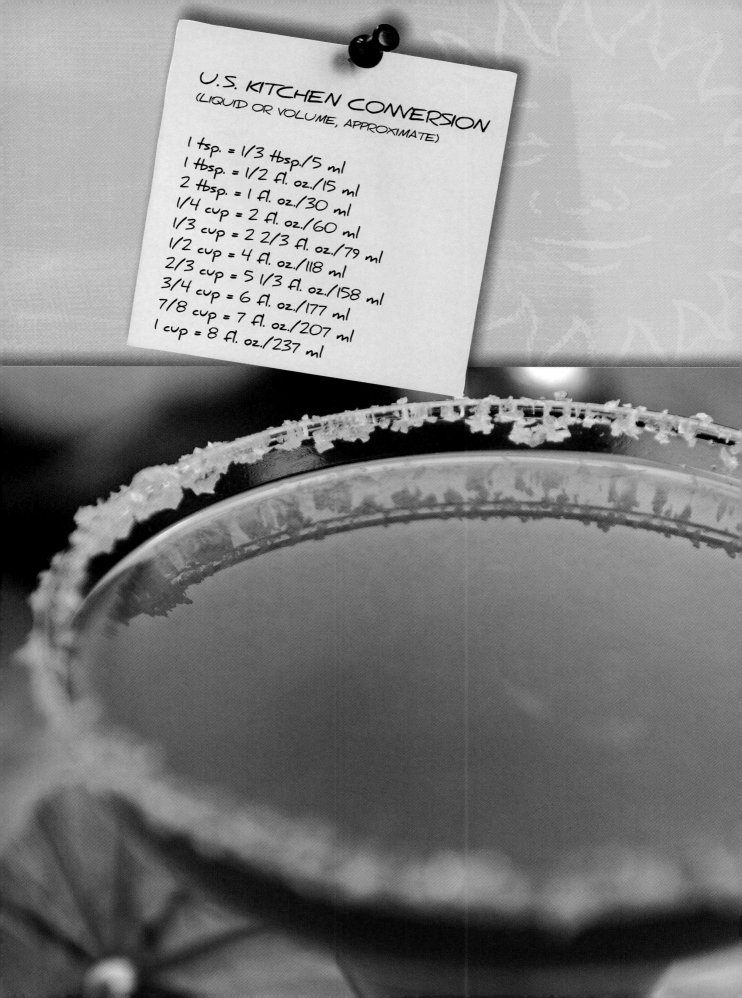

Traditional
Margarita

PREPARATION

The traditional margarita is based on a 3–2–1 principle:
3 parts tequila, 2 parts Cointreau, 1 part freshly squeezed lime
juice, shaken with ice and strained into a margarita glass.

Rub margarita glass rim with lemon slice and frost with salt.
Combine liquid ingredients with ice; shake well. Strain drink
into glass. Garnish with slice of lemon and serve.

INGREDIENTS

lemon slice
salt
1½ oz. (45 ml) tequila
1 oz. (30 ml) Cointreau
½ oz. (15 ml) lime juice, freshly
squeezed
ice
extra lemon slice, to garnish

Apple Margarita

PREPARATION

Rub margarita glass rims with lemon slice
and frost with salt.

Combine liquid ingredients with ice; shake well.
Strain drink into prepared glasses.
Garnish each glass with a lemon slice and serve.

INGREDIENTS

lemon slice
salt
1 oz. (30 ml) tequila
1 oz. (30 ml) Calvados
1 oz. (30 ml) Grand Marnier Rouge
1 oz. (30 ml) grenadine
ice
extra lemon slices, to garnish

Banana Margarita

PREPARATION

Rub margarita glass rim with lime or lemon slice
and frost with salt.

Combine liquid ingredients with ice; shake well.
Strain drink into glass.

Garnish with banana slice and serve.

INGREDIENTS

lemon or lime slice
salt

1 oz. (30 ml) banana liqueur
1/2 oz. (15 ml) Cointreau
11/2 oz. (45 ml) tequila
1 oz. (30 ml) lime or lemon juice
ice

banana slice, to garnish

Blackberry Margarita

PREPARATION

Rub margarita glass rim with lime or lemon slice and frost with salt.

Combine liquid ingredients with ice; shake well. Strain drink into glass.

Garnish with lime wedge and serve.

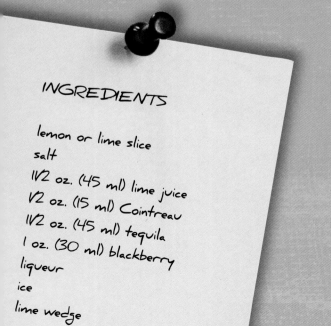

INGREDIENTS

lemon or lime slice
salt
1½ oz. (45 ml) lime juice
½ oz. (15 ml) Cointreau
1½ oz. (45 ml) tequila
1 oz. (30 ml) blackberry liqueur
ice
lime wedge

Blackcurrant
Margarita

PREPARATION

Rub margarita glass rim with lime or lemon slice
and frost with salt.

Combine liquid ingredients with ice; shake well.
Strain drink into glass.

Garnish with lime wedge and serve.

INGREDIENTS

lemon or lime slice

salt

1½ oz. (45 ml) lime juice

½ oz. (15 ml) Cointreau

1½ oz. (45 ml) tequila

1 oz. (30 ml) crème de cassis liqueur

ice

lime wedge, to garnish

Blue Margarita

Makes 2 servings

PREPARATION

Prepare glasses by rubbing margarita glass rims with lime slice and frosting with salt. Fill a cocktail shaker halfway with ice. Place tequila, triple sec, lime juice, Blue Curacao, and sugar in the shaker; shake hard for 30 seconds.

Fill the prepared glasses with ice cubes. Garnish each with a slice of star fruit or a lime wedge.

INGREDIENTS

lime slice
1 tsp. coarse salt
ice cubes
4 oz. (125 ml) tequila
1 oz. (30 ml) triple sec
2 oz. (60 ml) lime juice
2 oz. (60 ml) Blue Curacao
1 tsp. superfine sugar
2¼-inch (5 1/2 cm) slices star fruit
1 lime, cut into wedges

Cadillac Margarita

PREPARATION

Prepare glasses by rubbing margarita glass rims with lime slice and frosting with salt. Shake tequila with Grand Marnier and lime juice, and strain into a prepared cocktail glass.

Garnish with lime wedge.

INGREDIENTS

lime slice
salt
1½ oz. (45 ml) tequila
1 oz. (30 ml) Grand Marnier
⅓ oz (10 ml) lime juice
lime wedge, to garnish

Catalina Margarita

Makes 8 cups

20

PREPARATION

To make Sweet and Sour Mix: Combine water and sugar
in a large saucepan. Stir over medium heat until sugar
dissolves. Bring to a boil. Cool syrup. Mix syrup, lemon juice,
and lime juice in a pitcher and chill until cold.
(Can be made 1 week ahead. Cover; keep chilled.)

Prepare glasses by rubbing margarita glass rim with lime slice
and frosting with salt. Mix all liquid ingredients with cracked
ice in a shaker or blender and strain into the chilled prepared
margarita glass. Garnish with a lime wedge.

INGREDIENTS

lime slice

salt

1 1/2 oz. (45 ml) gold tequila

1 oz. (30 ml) peach schnapps

1 oz. (30 ml) Blue Curacao

4 oz. (125 ml) Sweet and Sour Mix (see page 20)

ice

lime wedge, to garnish

SWEET AND SOUR MIX

3 cups (24 fl. oz./710 ml) water

3 cups (600 g) granulated sugar

2 cups (16 fl. oz./473 ml) fresh lemon juice

2 cups (16 fl. oz./473 ml) fresh lime juice

Chambord Margarita

PREPARATION

Rub margarita glass rim with lime or lemon slice and frost with salt. Combine liquid ingredients with ice; shake well.

Strain drink into glass. Garnish with lime quarter and serve.

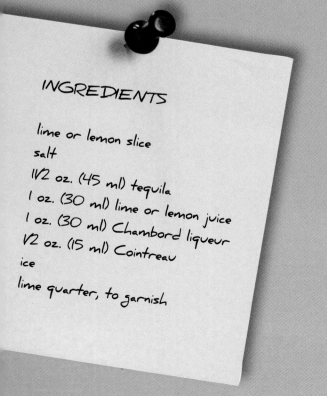

INGREDIENTS

lime or lemon slice
salt
1½ oz. (45 ml) tequila
1 oz. (30 ml) lime or lemon juice
1 oz. (30 ml) Chambord liqueur
½ oz. (15 ml) Cointreau
ice
lime quarter, to garnish

Cherry Margarita

PREPARATION

Rub margarita glass rim with lime or lemon slice and frost with salt. Combine liquid ingredients with ice; shake well.

Strain drink into glass.
Garnish with lime wedge and serve.

INGREDIENTS

lime or lemon slice
salt

1½ oz. (45 ml) tequila
1 oz. (30 ml) maraschino liqueur
1½ oz. (45 ml) lime juice, freshly squeezed
½ oz. (15 ml) Cointreau
ice

lime wedge, to garnish

Citrus Margarita

PREPARATION

Rub margarita glass rim with lime or lemon slice
and frost with salt. Combine liquid ingredients
with ice; shake well.

Strain drink into glass.
Garnish with orange slice and serve.

INGREDIENTS

lime or lemon slice
salt
2 oz. (60 ml) tequila
1 oz. (30 ml) lime juice, freshly
squeezed
1 oz. (30 ml) orange juice, freshly
squeezed
1 oz. (30 ml) Cointreau
ice

orange slice, to garnish

Cowboy Margarita

Makes about 4 big servings

INGREDIENTS

1½ cups (12 fl. oz./355 ml) frozen limeade concentrate

1½ cups (12 fl. oz./355 ml) tequila

1½ cups (12 fl. oz./355 ml) beer

ice

PREPARATION

Place undiluted frozen limeade concentrate in a pitcher. Fill empty limeade can with tequila and pour into the pitcher. Fill empty limeade can with beer and pour into the pitcher. Serve over plenty of ice.

Cranberry Margarita

PREPARATION

Rub margarita glass rim with lemon slice
and frost with sugar. Combine liquid ingredients
with ice; shake well. Pour drink into glass.
Garnish with lemon slice and serve.

INGREDIENTS

lemon slice
3/4 oz. (25 ml) triple sec
granulated sugar
2 1/2 oz. (75 ml) cranberry juice
1 1/2 oz. (45 ml) tequila
3/4 oz. (25 ml) lemon juice
5 ice cubes
lemon slices, extra, to garnish

Gold Margarita

PREPARATION

Rub margarita glass rim with lime or lemon slice
and frost with salt. Combine liquid ingredients with ice;
shake well. Strain drink into glass.
Garnish with lime wedge and serve.

INGREDIENTS

lime or lemon slice
salt
1/2 oz. (15 ml) Cointreau
2 oz. (60 ml) gold tequila
1 1/2 oz. (45 ml) lime juice
ice
lime wedge, to garnish

Frozen Cherry Margaritas

Makes 2–4 cocktails

INGREDIENTS

lime or lemon slice
salt
6 maraschino cherries
1½ oz. (45 ml) tequila
sugar, to taste
1 oz. (30 ml) lime juice
1 oz. (30 ml) maraschino liqueur
ice
extra lime or lemon slices,
to garnish

PREPARATION

Rub margarita glass rims with lime or lemon slice
and frost with salt. In a blender, combine maraschino
cherries, tequila, sugar, lime juice, and maraschino
liqueur. Blend until smooth.

Add ice cubes a few at a time until
the mixture becomes thick and slushy.
Pour into prepared glasses.
Garnish with lime or lemon slice and serve.

Frozen Double Apricot Margarita

Makes 2–4 margarita cocktails

INGREDIENTS

lime or lemon slice
coarse salt
1¼ cups (200 g) halved,
pitted, unpeeled apricots
or 1 lb. (500 g) canned unpeeled
apricot halves (drained)
¼ cup (2 fl. oz./60 ml)
tequila
2 oz. (60 ml) granulated sugar

2 oz. (60 ml) lime juice
2 oz. (60 ml) apricot nectar
3 cups ice cubes
extra lime juice
lime or lemon slices, extra, to garnish

PREPARATION

Rub margarita glass rims with lime or lemon slice
and frost with salt. In a blender, combine apricot
halves, tequila, sugar, lime juice, and apricot nectar.
Blend until smooth.

Add ice cubes a few at a time until
the mixture becomes thick and slushy.
Pour into prepared glasses.
Garnish with lime or lemon slice and serve.

Honeydew
Margarita

Makes 2–4 cocktails

PREPARATION

Rub margarita glass rims with lime slice
and frost with salt.

Blend melon, tequila, triple sec, lime juice,
and ice cubes until slushy.

Pour into prepared glasses, and garnish
each glass with a lime wedge.

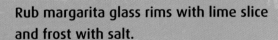

INGREDIENTS

3 cups (530 g) diced ripe honeydew melon
1/4 cup (2 fl. oz./60 ml) gold tequila
2 oz. (60 ml) triple sec
2 oz. (60 ml) lime juice
14 large ice cubes
6 lime wedges, to garnish

Frozen Strawberry Margarita

Makes 4 cocktails

PREPARATION

Rub margarita glass rims with lime or lemon slices
and frost with salt. Combine ingredients
in a blender and process until slushy.

Pour drink into prepared glasses.
Garnish with lime or lemon slice and serve.

INGREDIENTS

lime or lemon slices

1/4 cup (2 fl. oz./60 ml) frozen limeade concentrate

salt

1 cup (100 g) frozen strawberries

3/4 cup (6 fl. oz./175 ml) tequila

8 cups crushed ice

2 oz. (60 ml) triple sec

Non-Alcoholic Margarita Punch

Serves 20

INGREDIENTS

lemon or lime slice, salt

1½ cups (12 fl. oz./355 ml) frozen limeade concentrate

1½ cups (12 fl. oz./355 ml) frozen lemonade concentrate

1 cup (125 g) powdered sugar

equivalent of 4 egg whites (meringue powder)

6 cups crushed ice

8 cups (3 1/3 pints/1 liter, 30 oz.) lemon-lime soda, 1 lime, thinly sliced

1 lemon, thinly sliced

PREPARATION

Don't leave the kids out of the fiesta! Make this fun and festive punch for them and other teetotallers. It's a great all-purpose punch that works perfectly with Mexican menus, grilled food, and any outdoor gathering. Instead of using egg whites, we now use meringue powder to make sure the punch is safe from any possible contamination with salmonella.

Prepare glasses by rubbing margarita glass rims with lime or lemon slice and frosting with salt. Combine the concentrates, powdered sugar, egg whites or meringue powder, and crushed ice in a large freezer-proof container. Cover tightly and freeze for at least one hour and up to a month. Place the frozen mixture into a large punch bowl. Slowly pour in the soda and add the lime and lemon slices.

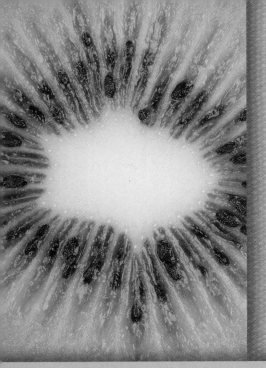

Kiwi Margarita

PREPARATION

Rub margarita glass rims with lime slices
and frost with salt. Put liquid ingredients, sugar,
and kiwifruit into a blender. On top of this
mixture, pour crushed ice until blender is full.

Blend until slushy. Pour into margarita glasses
and garnish each with a lime wedge.

INGREDIENTS

lime slices, salt

1/2 cup (4 fl. oz./125 ml) silver tequila

1/2 cup (4 fl. oz./125 ml) triple sec

1 cup (8 fl. oz./237 ml) lemon juice, freshly squeezed

1/2 cup (4 fl. oz./125 ml) lime juice, freshly squeezed

1/2 cup (65 g) powdered sugar

2 kiwi fruit, peeled

crushed ice, lime wedges, to garnish

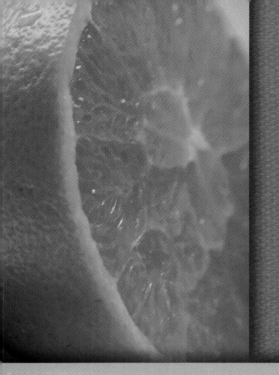

Acapulco

PREPARATION

Shake liquid ingredients with ice and strain into a 10-ounce (285 ml) hi-ball glass. Serve garnished with an orange slice.

INGREDIENTS

1 oz. (30 ml) tequila
5 oz. (150 ml) coconut cream
1 oz. (30 ml) dark rum
1 oz. (30 ml) Tia Maria
ice cubes
orange slice, to garnish

Bloody Maria

PREPARATION

In a shaker half-filled with ice, combine all of the ingredients except the garnish. Shake well and strain into a highball glass almost filled with ice cubes.

Garnish with a celery stalk and a straw.

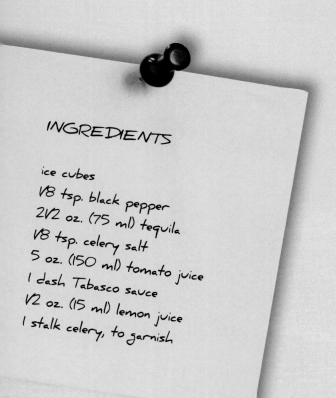

INGREDIENTS

ice cubes
1/8 tsp. black pepper
2 1/2 oz. (75 ml) tequila
1/8 tsp. celery salt
5 oz. (150 ml) tomato juice
1 dash Tabasco sauce
1/2 oz. (15 ml) lemon juice
1 stalk celery, to garnish

Earthquake

PREPARATION

Combine all ingredients except garnishes in a blender for 15 seconds. Strain cocktail into a champagne glass and garnish with a lime slice and strawberry.

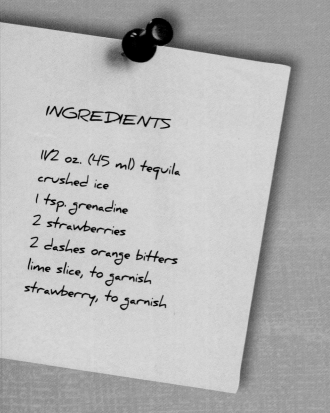

INGREDIENTS

1½ oz. (45 ml) tequila
crushed ice
1 tsp. grenadine
2 strawberries
2 dashes orange bitters
lime slice, to garnish
strawberry, to garnish

Exorcist

PREPARATION

Combine all ingredients except garnish in a shaker, shake, and strain into a 5-ounce (150 ml) cocktail glass. Garnish with half a lime slice.

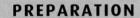

INGREDIENTS

1½ oz. (45 ml) tequila
3/4 oz. (25 ml) lime juice,
freshly squeezed
3/4 oz. (25 ml) Blue Curacao
½ lime slice, to garnish

Gates of Hell

PREPARATION

Combine all ingredients except
cherry brandy in a shaker. Shake well.

Strain into an old-fashioned glass
almost filled with crushed ice.
Drizzle the cherry brandy over the top.

INGREDIENTS

1½ oz. (45 ml) tequila
2 tsp. lemon juice, freshly
squeezed
2 tsp. lime juice, freshly
squeezed
crushed ice
1 tsp cherry brandy,
for drizzling

Gorilla Sweat

PREPARATION

Combine sugar and tequila into an old-fashioned glass. Add boiling water and pat of butter, and top with a shake of nutmeg.

INGREDIENTS

1/2 tsp. sugar
1 1/2 oz. (45 ml) tequila
boiling water
a pat of butter
ground nutmeg

Icebreaker

PREPARATION

Combine all ingredients in a blender and blend
for a few seconds. Strain into a margarita glass.

INGREDIENTS

2 oz. (60 ml) tequila
2 oz. (60 ml) grapefruit juice
1 tsp. grenadine
1/2 oz. (15 ml) Cointreau
crushed ice

Latin Lover

PREPARATION

Combine all ingredients in a shaker
and shake well. Strain into
an ice-filled old-fashioned glass.

INGREDIENTS

1V2 oz. (45 ml) champagne
(or sparkling wine)
2 tsp. lemon juice, freshly squeezed
3 dashes grenadine
1 oz. (30 ml) tequila
crushed ice

Mexican Flag

INGREDIENTS

2 oz. (60 ml) tequila
2 tsp. sugar syrup (see right)
2 tsp. lime juice, freshly squeezed
crushed ice, green, white,
and red cocktail onions,
to garnish

SUGAR SYRUP

2 oz. (60 ml) water
1 cup (200 g) sugar

PREPARATION

To make the sugar syrup, place sugar and water in a saucepan and bring to a boil. Reduce heat and simmer gently for approximately 5 minutes until the mixture condenses into a clear, sweet syrup. Cool. Use immediately or store indefinitely in a sealed container in the refrigerator.

Combine all ingredients except garnish in a shaker and shake well. Pour into a champagne glass. Garnish with green, white, and red cocktail onions on a toothpick across the glass.

Mexican Runner

PREPARATION

Blend all ingredients except garnish together and pour into a 10-ounce (285 ml) cocktail glass. Garnish with strawberry and umbrella.

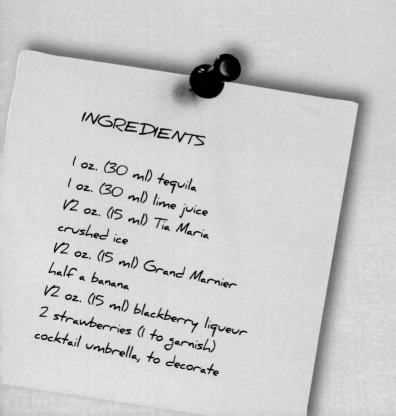

INGREDIENTS

1 oz. (30 ml) tequila
1 oz. (30 ml) lime juice
1/2 oz. (15 ml) Tia Maria
crushed ice
1/2 oz. (15 ml) Grand Marnier
half a banana
1/2 oz. (15 ml) blackberry liqueur
2 strawberries (1 to garnish)
cocktail umbrella, to decorate

Midori Matador

Makes 2 cocktails

PREPARATION

Combine all ingredients, except garnish, in a cocktail shaker and shake well. Fill two 8-ounce (250 ml) cocktail glasses with ice cubes.

Strain the cocktail into the glasses evenly. Squeeze a lemon wedge into each glass and then drop the wedge into the glass to serve.

INGREDIENTS

3 oz. (90 ml) Midori
2 tsp. powdered sugar
2 oz. (60 ml) silver tequila
crushed ice
1 oz. (30 ml) triple sec
3 oz. (90 ml) lemon juice
2 lemon wedges, to garnish

Mount Temple

PREPARATION

Build over ice in a 3-ounce (90 ml) cocktail glass.
Garnish with a dollop of cream in the center.

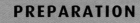

INGREDIENTS

ice

1 oz. (30 ml) Kahlua
1 oz. (30 ml) tequila
1 oz. (30 ml) coconut liqueur
dollop of thick cream, to garnish

Grilled Sea Scallops on Romaine Spears

Makes 12 pieces

INGREDIENTS

1–1½ lb. (450–650 g) sea scallops
(approximately 12 scallops)
¼ cup (45 g) couscous,
cooked and fluffed
3 tbsp. orange juice
2 tbsp. olive oil
3 cups mixed baby romaine spears
2 blood oranges, peeled
and segmented
(squeeze and reserve juice)

2 oz. (60 g) baby green beans,
cleaned and cooked
1 large tomato, cored and diced
fresh cracked black pepper
to taste

PREPARATION

Coat scallops in cooked couscous. Season and grill scallops.
Set aside and allow to cool.
In a mixing bowl, combine orange juice and olive oil.

Line up romaine spears, top with sea scallops, blood orange
segments, green beans, and tomato. Season with fresh
black cracked pepper and drizzle with dressing.

Spanish Chicken Drumettes with Chorizo

Makes 8 small servings

PREPARATION

Place chicken pieces in a large, non-stick frying pan and fry without oil for 5–8 minutes, turning occasionally, until golden. Remove chicken and set aside, then pour off any fat from the pan. Add oil to the pan and fry shallots, garlic, and bell pepper for 3–4 minutes, until softened.

Return chicken to the pan with the paprika, sherry or vermouth, tomatoes, bay leaf, and orange rind. Bring to a boil and simmer, covered, over low heat for 35–40 minutes, stirring occasionally, until chicken is cooked through. Add chorizo and olives and simmer for a further 5 minutes to heat through. Season with salt and pepper. Place 2 chicken pieces, with chorizo and pan ingredients, onto 4 plates.

INGREDIENTS

8 jointed chicken pieces, such as thighs
and drumsticks
2 tbsp. olive oil
6 shallots, sliced
2 cloves garlic, crushed
1 red and 1 yellow bell pepper, deseeded
and sliced
2 tsp. paprika
1/4 cup (2 fl. oz./60 ml) dry sherry
or dry vermouth
14 oz. (400 g) canned chopped tomatoes

1 bay leaf
1 strip orange rind, pared
with a vegetable peeler
2 1/2 oz. (75 g) chorizo,
sliced
2 oz. (60 g) pitted black
olives
salt and black pepper
to taste

Duck with Olives and Sherry

Makes 10 small servings

PREPARATION

Put olives in a small bowl, cover with warm water, and set aside.
Preheat the oven to 350°F/180°C. Sprinkle duck with salt and pepper.
Place it in a roasting pan and prick it all over with a fork.
Roast for 1 hour.

Meanwhile, heat oil in a shallow flameproof casserole dish
and sauté onion, carrots, and garlic over medium-high heat
until onion has wilted. Cut duck into serving pieces.
Transfer the pieces to the casserole.

Pour off the fat in the roasting pan and deglaze the pan with chicken
stock, scraping up any particles stuck to the bottom.
Strain the liquid into the casserole.

Drain olives and add to the casserole along with sherry, thyme,
parsley, and salt and pepper. Bring to a boil on top of the stove,
and then cover and cook in the oven for 1 hour.

INGREDIENTS

½ cup (70 g) large Spanish green olives, sliced or chopped
4 duck breasts, as much fat removed as possible
salt and freshly ground pepper
1 tbsp. olive oil
1 medium onion, finely chopped
2 carrots, finely chopped
3 cloves garlic, minced
¾ cup (6 fl. oz./175 ml) chicken stock

¼ cup (2 fl. oz./60 ml) dry sherry or white wine
¼ tsp. fresh thyme
1 tbsp. parsley, minced

Beef Braised in Rioja

Makes 8 small servings

INGREDIENTS

3 tbsp. olive oil
1 1/2 lb. (24 oz./680 g) stewing beef, trimmed of fat and cut into 2 1/2 inch (6 cm) chunks
6 shallots, finely chopped
2 cloves garlic, crushed
2 stalks celery, thickly sliced
11 oz. (310 g) mushrooms, thickly sliced
1/2 tsp. ground allspice
1/2 bottle full-bodied red wine
1 cup (8 fl. oz./237 ml) tomato purée
2 sprigs fresh thyme
salt and black pepper

PREPARATION

Preheat the oven to 350ºF/180°C. Heat oil in a flameproof casserole dish or large saucepan and fry meat over high heat, stirring, for 5-10 minutes or until browned. Remove from the pan.

Add shallots, garlic, and celery to pan and cook, stirring, for 3-4 minutes, until lightly browned. Add mushrooms and cook for 1 minute or until softened. Stir in allspice, wine, tomato purée, and 1 sprig of thyme, and season with salt and pepper. Return meat to the dish or pan and bring to a simmer.

Cover and cook in the oven or over a low heat on the stove for 1½ –2 hours, until beef is tender. Season again if necessary, and serve garnished with remaining thyme.

Chicken Meatballs with Sweet Chili Sauce

Makes about 30 small meatballs

PREPARATION

Place ground chicken in a bowl and add salt, breadcrumbs, onion, cilantro, curry paste, and egg. Mix together very well with a wooden spoon. Let rest for 10–20 minutes before shaping.

Take a heaped teaspoon of mixture and, with wet hands, roll into a ball and repeat until all balls are made. Place on a tray ready to fry. Mix flour and seasoning together; sprinkle onto a flat plate or sheet of parchment paper.

Heat oil in a wide heavy-based frying pan. Roll each meatball in the flour; shake off excess, and place in pan. Do not crowd pan, and adjust heat where necessary to fry at a steady pace. Turn meatballs frequently and roll while frying to keep a good round shape. Remove as they cook and drain on paper towels.

Serve chicken meatballs on a platter and provide the sweet chili sauce in a bowl for dipping.

INGREDIENTS

1 lb. (500 g) ground chicken
1/2 tsp. salt
1/4 cup (30 g) dried breadcrumbs
1 medium onion, finely chopped
1 tbsp. chopped cilantro
1 tbsp. mild curry paste
1 egg
1 cup (125 g) all-purpose flour

1/2 tsp. salt and pepper combined
1/4 cup (2 fl. oz./60 ml) canola oil
1/2 cup (4 fl. oz./125 ml) sweet chili sauce for dipping

Spinach, Olive, and Feta Frittata

Makes 16–18 pieces

INGREDIENTS

10 eggs

1 tbsp. fresh oregano, chopped

black pepper, freshly cracked

1/4 cup (2 fl. oz./60 ml) olive oil

7 oz. (200 g) potatoes, peeled and diced

1 brown onion, diced

1 clove garlic, crushed

5 oz. (150 g) baby spinach

2 oz. (60 g) pitted Kalamata olives, halved

2 oz. (60 g) feta cheese, crumbled

2 oz. (60 g) semi-dried tomatoes

3 large red bell peppers

PREPARATION

Lightly whisk together the eggs and oregano in a bowl, and season with black pepper. Set aside. Heat the oil in an 8 ¾ inch (22 cm) pan and sauté the potatoes, onion, and garlic for a few minutes until soft. Add the spinach and cook until it begins to wilt. Remove the pan from the heat.

Add olives, feta cheese, and semi-dried tomatoes. Return the pan to very low heat, pour in the egg mixture, and cook for 10–15 minutes. Run a spatula around the sides of the pan as the frittata is cooking, and tilt it slightly so that egg mixture runs down the sides a little.

When frittata is almost cooked through the middle, place under a grill for 5 minutes to cook and brown the top. Cut in wedges or squares with a drizzle of the roasted red-pepper sauce on top.

For Red-Pepper Sauce: halve the red bell peppers and remove the seeds. Grill or broil the peppers until black. Let them cool, and remove the skins. Place into a food processor and process until puréed. Transfer to a bowl. Makes ½ cup (4 fl. oz./125 ml).

Shrimp
with Spinach

PREPARATION

Heat two tablespoons olive oil in a saucepan, and brown onion.
Add red bell pepper, garlic, and tomatoes, and cook for 7 minutes.
Add spinach, white wine, lemon juice, and seasoning.
Cover and simmer gently for 8–10 minutes until spinach is tender.
Remove from heat. Stir and keep warm.

Add the remaining oil to a large frying pan. Once hot, add shrimp
and sauté, stirring constantly, for 3 minutes or until just cooked.
Spoon the shrimp into the spinach mixture, fold to combine,
and spoon onto a warm serving platter garnished with lemon
wedges. Serve immediately.

INGREDIENTS

3½ oz. (100 ml) olive oil
1 medium onion, diced
1 red bell pepper, deseeded and diced
1 clove garlic, crushed
2 tomatoes, peeled and diced
1½ bunches baby spinach, washed
and roughly chopped
2 tbsp. dry white wine
juice of 1 lemon
salt and freshly ground black pepper

1 lb. (500 g) shrimp, shelled
and deveined
lemon wedges, to garnish

Lemon Chicken Fingers

Serves 4

INGREDIENTS

2 lb. (1 kg) chicken breast filets
oil for deep frying

MARINADE

2 tbsp. soy sauce
1/4 cup (2 fl. oz./60 ml) sherry
2 tsp. grated fresh ginger
2 tsp. lemon zest
2 tsp. sugar

BATTER

2 egg whites
1/4 cup (30 g) all-purpose flour
1/4 cup (2 fl. oz./60 ml) lemon juice

DIPPING SAUCE

reserved marinade
1/2 cup (4 fl. oz./125 ml) chicken stock
2 tbsp. lemon juice, 2 tbsp. cornstarch

PREPARATION

Cut the breast filets into ⅜-inch (1 cm) wide strips from the long side of the filet. Place strips in a non-metal dish. Combine marinade ingredients, pour over chicken strips, mix well, and allow to marinate for 30 minutes.

To make the batter, stiffly beat the egg whites to soft peaks, and fold in flour and lemon juice. Remove the strips from marinade, reserving the marinade.

Heat oil in a deep fryer to 350°F/180°C. Dip a few strips at a time into the batter and deep fry them for 5 minutes until golden. Drain on paper towels. Repeat with remainder.

Pour reserved marinade into a saucepan, add chicken stock, and bring to a boil. Mix the lemon juice and cornstarch into a smooth paste, stir into the saucepan, lower heat, and stir until sauce boils and thickens.

Drizzle sauce over chicken fingers and serve.

Baby Octopus Marinated in Olive Oil and Oregano

Serves 4

PREPARATION

In a bowl, mix together the olive oil, lemon zest, lemon juice, shallots, oregano, and pepper and salt. Add the octopus, and leave to marinate for 1 hour.

Heat a chargrill/broiler pan, lightly brush with oil, add octopus, and cook, basting with marinade for 2–3 minutes, or until tender. Serve on a bed of salad leaves.

INGREDIENTS

1/3 cup (2 1/2 fl. oz./75 ml) olive oil
zest of 1 lemon
2 tbsp. lemon juice
5 tbsp. (50 g) shallots, finely sliced
2 tsp. oregano, chopped
freshly ground black pepper and salt
1 1/2 lb. (750 g) baby octopus, cleaned
lettuce leaves, for serving

Marinated Calamari with Lemon and Herb Dressing

Serves 4–6

PREPARATION

Place lemon juice, garlic, and oil in a bowl.
Add the calamari, and marinate for at least 3 hours.
If time permits, marinate overnight.

To make the dressing, place all ingredients in a bowl
or jar and whisk well, until dressing thickens slightly.
Heat 1 tablespoon oil in a pan, add the calamari,
and cook for a few minutes, until calamari are cooked through.
Alternatively, the calamari can be cooked on a chargrill/broiler.
Serve calamari with lemon and herb dressing drizzled over.

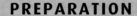

INGREDIENTS

3 oz. (90 ml) lemon juice
3 cloves garlic, crushed
1/2 cup (4 fl. oz./125 ml) olive oil, extra
for cooking
2 lb. (1 kg) calamari, cut into thin rings

DRESSING

2 oz. (60 ml) lemon juice
3 1/2 oz. (100 ml) olive oil
1 1/2 tbsp. parsley, chopped

1 garlic clove, crushed
1 tsp. Dijon mustard
salt and black pepper

Asparagus with Pecorino and Pancetta

Serves 4–6

INGREDIENTS

1 lb. (500 g) asparagus
8 thin slices of pancetta,
cut into pieces
pecorino cheese, shaved

DRESSING

juice of 1 lemon
3½ oz. (100 ml) extra-virgin olive oil
sea salt
black pepper, freshly ground

PREPARATION

Trim off the thick ends of the asparagus and cook in boiling water for 4 minutes, until tender but still crisp. Run under cold water, until asparagus is cool, and dry with paper towels.

For the dressing, place the lemon juice in a bowl and slowly add the oil, whisking, until dressing is thick. Season with salt and pepper. Pour the dressing over the asparagus, and serve with the pancetta and pecorino cheese shavings.

Potato Omelet

Serves 6-8

PREPARATION

Heat oil in a frying pan, add potatoes and onion, season, and cover.
Fry gently, moving the pan so that vegetables don't stick. Once potatoes
are cooked (take care they don't become crisp), break them up a bit
and remove from the pan with a slotted spoon. Add to the beaten eggs.
Stir potatoes around until they are well covered with egg.
Add salt to taste.

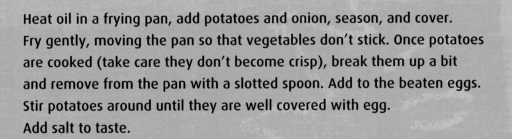

Remove most of the oil from the frying pan, leaving about 1 tablespoon
oil, and reheat. Have handy a plate with a slightly larger diameter
than the pan. Return egg and potato mixture to the pan and cook
for a few minutes until one side is golden.

Next (and this is slightly tricky), slip the omelet out onto the plate,
cooked-side down, and then slip it back into the pan, cooked-side up.
Cook until firm. Your omelet should be about 1 ½ inches (4 cm) thick.
If you are using it for tapas, cut it into squares.

INGREDIENTS

2 lb. (1 kg) potatoes, peeled and sliced thinly
1 small onion, peeled and diced finely (optional)
1 cup (8 fl. oz./237 ml) olive oil
5 eggs, beaten
salt

Sesame Twists

PREPARATION

Cut the puff-pastry sheets in half. Brush with melted butter.
Combine the poppy seeds, sesame seeds, and cheese,
and sprinkle over pastry. Press the seeds firmly
into the pastry with a rolling pin.

Using a sharp knife, cut widthwise into strips three-quarters
of an inch (2 cm) wide and 4 inches (10 cm) long.
Twist strips slightly. Place onto a lightly greased baking
tray and bake in a hot oven, 350°F/180°C, for 8 minutes.

INGREDIENTS

2 sheets of puff pastry
2 oz. (60 g) butter, melted
2 tbsp. poppy seeds
2 tbsp. sesame seeds
2 tbsp. grated Parmesan cheese

Index

drinks

appetizers